Quilt Art
'96

Engagement Calendar

*A collection of prize-winning
quilts from across the country.*

Another quality product from your American Quilter's Society.

Color photography by Richard Walker, Schenevus, New York.

On the cover:

CLOISONNE by Dorothy Erlenborn, Alexandria, VA. 65" x 80". Inspired by a doodle done by New York Congressman, Barber Conable who served in congress with Dorothy's husband. Fourth in a series of "doodle inspired" pieces. State winner in the Land's End All American Quilt Contest, Dodgeville, WI.

Quilt Art '96

Klaudeen Hansen

From Sun Prairie, Wisconsin, Klaudeen Hansen and Annette Riddle have spent years seeking the most beautiful quilts to include in the Quilt Art Engagement Calendars. And, the 1996 calendar promises to be some of the best work to date.

Annette, a quilt shop owner who travels to major quilt shows across the country, and Klaudeen, a quilt teacher and experienced quilt judge, both have the opportunity to view some of the most beautiful quilts in the world. They look for the up and coming quiltmakers who have not achieved national recognition yet, but are creating innovative and beautiful quilts. The map below shows where these talented quilt artists were found.

Quilt enthusiasts everywhere have enjoyed Annette's and Klaudeen's selections for more than 10 years. Many even refer to the calendar as a year round quilt show. So enjoy your personal exhibit they have prepared for you for 1996, and look for these quilt artists to be national successes in the next few years!

Annette Riddle

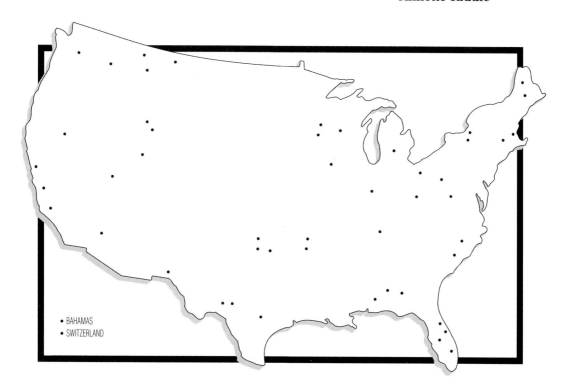

• BAHAMAS
• SWITZERLAND

JANUARY

1

TUESDAY

2

WEDNESDAY

3

THURSDAY

4

FRIDAY

5

ON THE FIRST DAY
by Emily Senuta, Overland Park, KS. 42" x 42". After reading about distorted blocks, Emily designed three sizes of Aunt Sukey's choice blocks. The Hoffman Challenge Fabric was the excuse to start and finish this piece. A winner at Quilts Unlimited, Kansas City, MO.

SATURDAY

6

SUNDAY

7

JANUARY

S	M	T	W	T	F	S
	1	2	3	4	5	6
7	8	9	10	11	12	13
14	15	16	17	18	19	20
21	22	23	24	25	26	27
28	29	30	31			

JANUARY

MONDAY
8

TUESDAY
9

WEDNESDAY
10

THURSDAY
11

FRIDAY
12

TIES ALL AROUND
by Brenda Smallwood-Horton, Fort Smith, AR. 50" in diameter. Each swatch in this cathedral window variation is different, including the prairie points – making it something of a charm quilt in flavor and a Victorian era crazy quilt in appearance. The antique black glass beads add a twinkle of light at each junction of the sashing.

SATURDAY
13

SUNDAY
14

JANUARY						
S	M	T	W	T	F	S
	1	2	3	4	5	6
7	8	9	10	11	12	13
14	15	16	17	18	19	20
21	22	23	24	25	26	27
28	29	30	31			

JANUARY

MONDAY   MARTIN LUTHER KING JR.'S BIRTHDAY OBSERVED
15

TUESDAY
16

WEDNESDAY
17

THURSDAY
18

FRIDAY
19

OUR TOWN
by Sandra Lynn Barford and quilted by Gert Gojeski, Doylestown, PA. 62" x 84". The inspiration for this folk art quilt came from many sources. Among them a concrete castle standing in the center of Sandra's town and deer crossing signs (she traced directly from them!). Displayed at the Variable Star Quilter's Show, Doylestown, PA.

SATURDAY
20

Party Lite Candle Party Debbie 's 130pm

SUNDAY
21

			JANUARY			
S	M	T	W	T	F	S
	1	2	3	4	5	6
7	8	9	10	11	12	13
14	15	16	17	18	19	20
21	22	23	24	25	26	27
28	29	30	31			

JANUARY

MONDAY
22

TUESDAY
23

WEDNESDAY
24 *PartyLite Candle Party - Javala's 7pm*

THURSDAY
25 *Babysit Dallas*

FRIDAY
26 *Babysit Dallas.*

BRODERIE PERSE MEDALLION
by Bettina Havig, Columbia, MO. 82" x 82". Original broderie perse appliqué center medallion is framed by scrap triangular blocks. Appliqué elements for central medallion are cut from the print used for the outer border. Displayed at Quilts Across America, Peoria, IL, and AQS.

SATURDAY
27

SUNDAY
28

			JANUARY			
S	M	T	W	T	F	S
	1	2	3	4	5	6
7	8	9	10	11	12	13
14	15	16	17	18	19	20
21	22	23	24	25	26	27
28	29	30	31			

JANUARY / FEBRUARY

MONDAY
29

TUESDAY
30

WEDNESDAY
31

THURSDAY
1

FRIDAY
2

A GIFT OF LOVE
by The Palm Beach County
Quilter's Guild and owned by Jeri
Hight, Lantana, FL.
76" x 77". This gift of love was
designed by Dory Sandon. It was
brought to fruition by Kathy Ward
and Sara McLennand. A first place
winner at Quilter's Heritage
Celebration, Lancaster, PA.

SATURDAY
3

SUNDAY
4

FEBRUARY						
S	M	T	W	T	F	S
				1	2	3
4	5	6	7	8	9	10
11	12	13	14	15	16	17
18	19	20	21	22	23	24
25	26	27	28	29		

FEBRUARY

MONDAY
5

TUESDAY
6

WEDNESDAY
7

THURSDAY
8

FRIDAY
9

CHALLENGE SAMPLER
by Catherine G. Daniel, Largo, FL.
63" x 63". A set of challenge
blocks Catherine won challenged
her setting skills. The end product
of a real drafting and constructon
experience is this unusual
sampler. Displayed at Quilted
Treasures, Clearwater, FL.

SATURDAY
10
Pads? Dado 9/10

SUNDAY
11

			FEBRUARY			
S	M	T	W	T	F	S
				1	2	3
4	5	6	7	8	9	10
11	12	13	14	15	16	17
18	19	20	21	22	23	24
25	26	27	28	29		

FEBRUARY

MONDAY   LINCOLN'S BIRTHDAY

12

TUESDAY

13

WEDNESDAY   ST. VALENTINE'S DAY

14

THURSDAY

15

FRIDAY

16

Lunch w/Bonnie - Drop Megan off at Debbie's

BEYOND A SECRET SUNRISE
by Deanne Bodeau-Mackinnon, Seattle, WA. 54" x 56". A distant light source defines the fragmented arrowhead block. Strip pieced shade of sun, sea, and sky. Metallic movement quilted in rays, waves, and currents. Displayed at the Great Pacific Northwest Quilt Show and Quilter's Anonymous, Monroe, WA.

SATURDAY

17

Dallas Party 12:30 - 1:00 Supper 4ish

SUNDAY

18

Cindy - Candle party 1:30

FEBRUARY

S	M	T	W	T	F	S
				1	2	3
4	5	6	7	8	9	10
11	12	13	14	15	16	17
18	19	20	21	22	23	24
25	26	27	28	29		

FEBRUARY

MONDAY   WASHINGTON'S BIRTHDAY OBSERVED

19

AGT moving cline babysit Dallas?

TUESDAY

20

WEDNESDAY   ASH WEDNESDAY

21

THURSDAY

22

ACLS - picking up clothes - leave on front step - Mark ACLS - Alberta Community Living Svc

FRIDAY

23

PASDE DEUX LA PAPPILLION
by Elsie Campbell, Arkansas City, KS. 36" in diameter. A skewed view of the traditional Log Cabin is represented in the circular piece. It won first place and viewer's choice in her guild's challenge and was displayed at the Walnut Valley Quilt Guild's Show.

SATURDAY

24

DONNA'S BD PARTY

SUNDAY

25

FEBRUARY

S	M	T	W	T	F	S
				1	2	3
4	5	6	7	8	9	10
11	12	13	14	15	16	17
18	19	20	21	22	23	24
25	26	27	28	29		

FEBRUARY / MARCH

MONDAY
26

TUESDAY
27

WEDNESDAY
28

THURSDAY
29

FRIDAY
1

FOREVER FLOWERS
by Marian K. Brockschmidt,
Springfield, IL. 75" x 75". Design
elements from a commercial
pattern line were used by
Marian's daughter to create this
piece. This quilt is a trophy
winner for best needlework at
the Illinois State Fair and was
shown at Quilts Across America,
Peoria, IL.

SATURDAY
2

Linda Party - light 3pm

SUNDAY
3

			MARCH			
S	M	T	W	T	F	S
					1	2
3	4	5	6	7	8	9
10	11	12	13	14	15	16
17	18	19	20	21	22	23
24	25	26	27	28	29	30
31						

MARCH

KALEIDOSCOPIC GARDEN by Maggie Ball, Bainbridge Island, WA. 84" x 84". Traditional design elements are used to produce an original design. The secondary pattern created is one of Maggie's favorite features of this piece. A winner at the Arkansas Quilters Guild Show and the Western Washington State Fair at Puyallup. She was also honored by her church when she did an exhibition of her work.

SATURDAY

9

SUNDAY

10

MARCH						
S	M	T	W	T	F	S
					1	2
3	4	5	6	7	8	9
10	11	12	13	14	15	16
17	18	19	20	21	22	23
24	25	26	27	28	29	30
31						

MARCH

MONDAY
11

TUESDAY
12

WEDNESDAY
13

THURSDAY
14

FRIDAY
15

THE SKY IS THE LIMIT
by Quilt Fan-Attics, Sylvania, OH.
93" x 109". From the kite theme
came this collection of both
traditional and original blocks.
"Luck of the draw" determined
the starting block for each
participant in this challenge.
Setting and hand quilting were
collaborative efforts. First place
winner at Sauder Farm & Village
Quilt Show, Archbold, OH, and
Expressions in Pieces Quilt
Show, Temperance, MI.

SATURDAY
16

NATIONAL QUILTING DAY

SUNDAY
17

ST. PATRICK'S DAY

MARCH

S	M	T	W	T	F	S
					1	2
3	4	5	6	7	8	9
10	11	12	13	14	15	16
17	18	19	20	21	22	23
24	25	26	27	28	29	30
31						

MARCH

MONDAY
18

TUESDAY
19

WEDNESDAY
20

THURSDAY
21

FRIDAY
22

JOSEPHINE'S GARDEN
by Wendy Richardson, Brooklyn Park, MN. 60" x 80". This quilt is the celebration of spring and the continuation of life. It is dedicated to her Aunt Jo and was a winner at the Minnesota State Fair Fine Arts Division and the Minnesota Quilter's State Convention.

SATURDAY
23

SUNDAY
24

MARCH

S	M	T	W	T	F	S
					1	2
3	4	5	6	7	8	9
10	11	12	13	14	15	16
17	18	19	20	21	22	23
24	25	26	27	28	29	30
31						

MARCH

TUESDAY
26

WEDNESDAY
27

THURSDAY
28

FRIDAY
29

LOOK, A GECKO!
by Marcelle Pellaton, Zurich, Switzerland. 40" x 60". Gecko is lizard in Swiss-German. The colors were inspired by the almost neon colors of the Bahamas and the many lizards which populate the islands. During the 4½ years spent in the islands, this was the first quilt she started and the last one finished. Displayed at Quilts Across America/Atlanta /Peoria and Stepping Stone Quilter's annual show, Nassau, Bahamas.

SATURDAY
30

SUNDAY
31

MARCH						
S	M	T	W	T	F	S
					1	2
3	4	5	6	7	8	9
10	11	12	13	14	15	16
17	18	19	20	21	22	23
24	25	26	27	28	29	30
31						

APRIL

MONDAY

1

TUESDAY

2

WEDNESDAY

3

THURSDAY   PASSOVER

4

FRIDAY   GOOD FRIDAY

5

RESURRECTION
by Dara Duffy Williamson,
Blowing Rock, NC. 39" x 55".
This quilt was commissioned by
Dara's father in memory of her
mother and will be given to a
church meaningful to the family
for display during the Easter
season each year. All cotton
fabrics, hand & machine pieced,
hand quilted in cotton and
metallic threads.

SATURDAY

6

SUNDAY   EASTER

7

				APRIL		
S	M	T	W	T	F	S
	1	2	3	4	5	6
7	8	9	10	11	12	13
14	15	16	17	18	19	20
21	22	23	24	25	26	27
28	29	30				

APRIL

MONDAY
8

TUESDAY
9

WEDNESDAY
10

THURSDAY
11

FRIDAY
12

TRELLIS OF SWEET PEAS
by Fairy D. Earnest, Orange, CA.
75" x 102". Quilting that echoes
the "sweet peas" provides textural
counterpoint for the trellis-look
quilting in the green strips.
Ribbon winner at the Prairie
Heritage Quilt Contest, Sun
Prairie, WI, and the Orange
County Fair, Orange, CA.

SATURDAY
13

SUNDAY
14

			APRIL			
S	M	T	W	T	F	S
	1	2	3	4	5	6
7	8	9	10	11	12	13
14	15	16	17	18	19	20
21	22	23	24	25	26	27
28	29	30				

APRIL

MONDAY

15

TUESDAY

16

WEDNESDAY

17

THURSDAY

18

FRIDAY

19

BIRDS OF A FEATHER #1
by Jan Brashears, Atlanta, GA.
45" x 46". An original design that
was transferred to paper
templates and was machine
pieced. Embellished with silk
and rayon threads to create
feather designs and shadings.
Displayed at the Aullwood
Audubon Show, Dayton, OH, and
NQA, Charleston, WV.

SATURDAY

20

SUNDAY

21

APRIL

S	M	T	W	T	F	S
	1	2	3	4	5	6
7	8	9	10	11	12	13
14	15	16	17	18	19	20
21	22	23	24	25	26	27
28	29	30				

APRIL

MONDAY
22

TUESDAY
23

WEDNESDAY
24

THURSDAY
25
 QUILT SHOW & CONTEST, PADUCAH, KY

FRIDAY
26
 QUILT SHOW & CONTEST

THE SUMMER BEFORE REALITY by Sharon Gilmore-Thompson, Lamoille, NV. 68" x 68". Precision piecing and metallic thread in the quilting are complements to the complex design surface. Unusual fabrics provide an exciting palette. Displayed at the Pacific International Quilt Show, San Francisco, CA.

SATURDAY
27
 QUILT SHOW & CONTEST

SUNDAY
28
 QUILT SHOW & CONTEST

APRIL						
S	M	T	W	T	F	S
	1	2	3	4	5	6
7	8	9	10	11	12	13
14	15	16	17	18	19	20
21	22	23	24	25	26	27
28	29	30				

APRIL / MAY

MONDAY
29

TUESDAY
30

WEDNESDAY
1

THURSDAY
2

FRIDAY
3

SATURDAY
4

SUNDAY
5

MY FANTASY GARDEN
by Claire Powers, Rockford, IL.
94" x 116". This original design
was made up to fit the theme of a
guild show. It took over 1000
hours to make, during an eight
month period. Best of Show at
both shows, Sinnissippi Quilt
Guild, Rockford, IL, and
Gingerbread & Calico Show,
Dekalb, IL.

			MAY			
S	M	T	W	T	F	S
				1	2	3	4
5	6	7	8	9	10	11
12	13	14	15	16	17	18
19	20	21	22	23	24	25
26	27	28	29	30	31	

MAY

MONDAY
6

TUESDAY
7

WEDNESDAY
8

THURSDAY
9

FRIDAY
10

SCRAPPY KALEIDOSCOPE
by Doris Heitman, Williamsburg, IA. 40" in diameter. This log cabin variation is completely machine made. It was pieced using the foundation method. Twin needle and metallic thread were used on the border which is also enhanced with meander quilting. A blue ribbon winner at the Iowa State Fair. It also took the Iowa Quilt Guild Award.

SATURDAY
11

SUNDAY
12

MOTHER'S DAY

MAY

S	M	T	W	T	F	S
			1	2	3	4
5	6	7	8	9	10	11
12	13	14	15	16	17	18
19	20	21	22	23	24	25
26	27	28	29	30	31	

MAY

MONDAY
13

TUESDAY
14

WEDNESDAY
15

THURSDAY
16

FRIDAY
17

DIAMOND CHARMS
by Helen Cogar, Las Cruces,
NM. 86" x 93". This traditionally
set charm quilt represents a
collection of 831 different pieces
of fabric from 18 different states
and 3 countries. A winner at
NQA, Charleston, WV.

SATURDAY   ARMED FORCES DAY
18

SUNDAY
19

			MAY			
S	M	T	W	T	F	S
				1	2	3	4
5	6	7	8	9	10	11
12	13	14	15	16	17	18
19	20	21	22	23	24	25
26	27	28	29	30	31	

MAY

20

TUESDAY
21

WEDNESDAY
22

THURSDAY
23

FRIDAY
24

ENCOMPASSING THE SEA
by Kathy Joray, Pine Bush, NY.
72" x 72". Mini Mariner's
Compasses anchor the Seminole
border that surround this Storm
at Sea. Machine pieced and
machine quilted. A winner at the
Northern Star World of Quilts
Show, NY.

SATURDAY
25

SUNDAY
26

			MAY			
S	M	T	W	T	F	S
			1	2	3	4
5	6	7	8	9	10	11
12	13	14	15	16	17	18
19	20	21	22	23	24	25
26	27	28	29	30	31	

MAY / JUNE

MONDAY   MEMORIAL DAY
27

TUESDAY
28

WEDNESDAY
29

THURSDAY
30

FRIDAY
31

TWILIGHT WREATH
by Marty Freed, Winterset, IA.
82" x 82". Best of Show and first
place in appliqué were awarded
to this traditionally hand-
appliquéd and hand-quilted piece
at the Iowa State Fair, Des
Moines, IA. Rose Kretziner's
quilts were Marty's design
inspiration.

SATURDAY
1

SUNDAY
2

			JUNE			
S	M	T	W	T	F	S
						1
2	3	4	5	6	7	8
9	10	11	12	13	14	15
16	17	18	19	20	21	22
23	24	25	26	27	28	29
30						

QUILT ART '97

Quilt Art '97 Engagement Calendar will be ready to ship by May 1, 1996. Please use this form to order your calendars anytime after May 1, 1996 (or order more *Quilt Art '96* calendars now). Calendar editors Klaudeen Hansen & Annette Riddle have another great group of 54 beautiful contemporary quilts to feature for your enjoyment!
Item #4597, 7 x 9, 112 Pgs. **$9.95**

QUILT ART '96

Don't you agree this *Quilt Art '96 Engagement Calendar* is really nice? Order now for your friends and family. These calendars make great gifts!
Item #3845, 7 x 9, 112 Pgs. **$9.95**

PLEASE SEND ME:

#4597 _____ copies of *Quilt Art '97 Engagement Calendar* @ $9.95 ...._____

#3845 _____ copies of *Quilt Art '96 Engagement Calendar* @ $9.95 ...._____

Add $1.00 per calendar for postage & handling ...._____

TOTAL ENCLOSED _____

SHIP TO:

☐ VISA ☐ MasterCard ☐ Check enclosed

Cardholder's Name _____

Card No. _____

Expiration date _____

Name _____

Address _____

City _____

State _____ Zip _____

VISA and MasterCard customers may also order TOLL-FREE (except Kentucky, Alaska & Hawaii) 1-800-626-5420, Mon.-Fri. 8:00 a.m. to 4:00 p.m. (CST). AQS office (502)898-7903.

American Quilter's Society
P.O. Box 3290
Paducah, KY 42002-3290

JUNE

MONDAY

3

TUESDAY

4

WEDNESDAY

5

THURSDAY

6

FRIDAY

7

COMPASS STAR
by Deborah DeRoche, Riverside, CA. 84" x 105". Traditional star medallion is surrounded by a spikey compass inner border. The yellow background is enhanced by intense feather cable quilting. First place winner at the Inland Empire Quilter's Guild Extravaganza, Riverside, CA.

SATURDAY

8

SUNDAY

9

			JUNE			
S	M	T	W	T	F	S
						1
2	3	4	5	6	7	8
9	10	11	12	13	14	15
16	17	18	19	20	21	22
23	24	25	26	27	28	29
30						

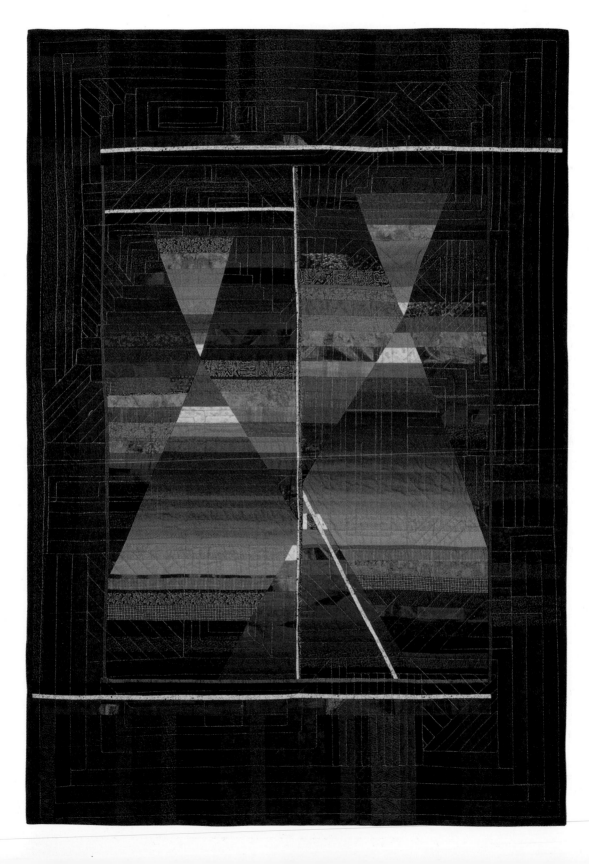

JUNE

MONDAY
10

TUESDAY
11

WEDNESDAY
12

THURSDAY
13

FRIDAY   FLAG DAY
14

OBELISK
by Karen Hull Sienk, Colden,
NY. 72" x 90". A watercolor
painting by Paul Klee was the
inspiration for this piece. This
was done for the "art challenge"
at Karen's guild. They were to
chose a favorite artist and either
reproduce one of their works or
work in their favorite's particular
style. Displayed at Quilts Across
America, Peoria, IL.

SATURDAY
15

SUNDAY   FATHER'S DAY
16

JUNE

MONDAY
17

TUESDAY
18

WEDNESDAY
19

THURSDAY
20

FRIDAY
21

GARDEN JEWELS
by Lisa Tan, Jan Rashid, La Jolla, CA, and The Canyon Quilters, San Diego, CA. 85" x 108". An exhibit of exotic butterflies at the San Diego Wild Animal Park inspired this kaleidoscopic view done in hand appliqué and embellished with hand embroidery. A ribbon winner at the Pacific International Quilt Festival, San Francisco, CA, and AIQA, Houston, TX.

SATURDAY
22

SUNDAY
23

JUNE

S	M	T	W	T	F	S
						1
2	3	4	5	6	7	8
9	10	11	12	13	14	15
16	17	18	19	20	21	22
23	24	25	26	27	28	29
30						

JUNE

MONDAY
24

TUESDAY
25

WEDNESDAY
26

THURSDAY
27

FRIDAY
28

RED SKY AT NIGHT
by Ellen Graf, Menasha, WI. 92" x 99". This is the first large quilt Ellen has made and it won a ribbon in the Founder's Division at NQA, Charleston, WV. It also won first place at the Darting Needles Guild Show, Appleton, WI.

SATURDAY
29

SUNDAY
30

			JUNE			
S	M	T	W	T	F	S
						1
2	3	4	5	6	7	8
9	10	11	12	13	14	15
16	17	18	19	20	21	22
23	24	25	26	27	28	29
30						

JULY

MONDAY

1

TUESDAY

2

WEDNESDAY

3

THURSDAY   **INDEPENDENCE DAY**

4

FRIDAY

5

INTERNATIONAL FABRICS III
by Barbara Butler, Marietta, GA.
80" x 100". A marriage of the
perfect fabric collection and the
perfect innovative setting of Baby
Bunting and Judy's Star blocks
meet in this totally American style.
Third in a series using international
fabrics. A state winner at the Land's
End All American Quilt Contest,
Dodgeville, WI.

SATURDAY

6

SUNDAY

7

JULY

S	M	T	W	T	F	S
	1	2	3	4	5	6
7	8	9	10	11	12	13
14	15	16	17	18	19	20
21	22	23	24	25	26	27
28	29	30	31			

JULY

MONDAY

8

TUESDAY

9

WEDNESDAY

10

THURSDAY

11

FRIDAY

12

EYE OF THE STORM
by Deanna D. Dison, Spearsville, LA. 78" x 92". Several variations of the traditional Log Cabin block were used to produce this innovative quilt. Color and setting also contribute to its style. Winner at the Columbus Heritage Quilt Show, Columbus, IN, and displayed at Quilt America, Indianapolis, IN.

SATURDAY

13

SUNDAY

14

JULY

S	M	T	W	T	F	S
	1	2	3	4	5	6
7	8	9	10	11	12	13
14	15	16	17	18	19	20
21	22	23	24	25	26	27
28	29	30	31			

JULY

SUNNY DAZE
by Chris Cunat, West Dundee, IL. 82" x 82". A new twist of an old favorite, this New York Beauty's border echoes its inner block design. Machine pieced and machine and hand quilted. Displayed at AQS.

SATURDAY
20

SUNDAY
21

JULY						
S	M	T	W	T	F	S
	1	2	3	4	5	6
7	8	9	10	11	12	13
14	15	16	17	18	19	20
21	22	23	24	25	26	27
28	29	30	31			

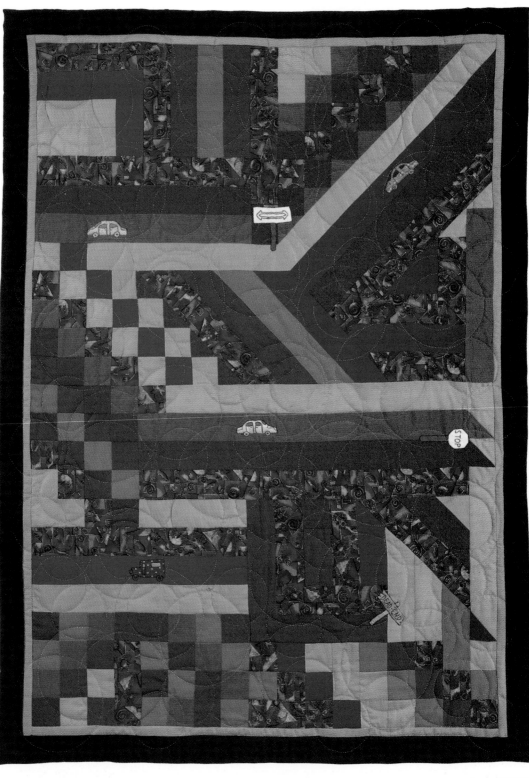

JULY

MONDAY

22

TUESDAY

23

WEDNESDAY

24

THURSDAY

25

FRIDAY

26

HIGHWAY TO NOWHERE
by Helen Beer, Solon, OH.
46" x 35". Helen was given this
design in a fabric dying class
taken years ago. While on a trip
to Australia she was reminded of
this pattern by one of their roads
to nowhere. This piece toured
with The Hoffman Challenge.

SATURDAY

27

SUNDAY

28

JULY

S	M	T	W	T	F	S
		1	2	3	4	5	6
7	8	9	10	11	12	13
14	15	16	17	18	19	20
21	22	23	24	25	26	27
28	29	30	31			

JULY / AUGUST

MONDAY
29

TUESDAY
30

WEDNESDAY
31

THURSDAY
1

FRIDAY
2

AZTEC SUNFLOWER
by Marabee J. Seifert, Easley, SC. 58" x 58". A design process demonstrated at a quilt guild meeting was the inspiration for this kaleidoscopic look. The original pattern was used as her challenge piece and it won first place. First place winner at Asheville Quilt Show, Asheville, NC, and Upcountry Guild Quilt Show, Liberty, SC.

SATURDAY
3

SUNDAY
4

AUGUST

S	M	T	W	T	F	S
					1	2	3
4	5	6	7	8	9	10
11	12	13	14	15	16	17
18	19	20	21	22	23	24
25	26	27	28	29	30	31

AUGUST

MONDAY
5

TUESDAY
6

WEDNESDAY
7

THURSDAY
8

FRIDAY
9

KANSAS SUNFLOWERS
by Rosie Grinstead, Mission Hills, KS. 45" x 45". Sunflower fabric was the inspiration for both color and design in this wall quilt. Swirling motion of the traditional Log Cabin blocks represent windmills. Winner at NQA, Charleston, WV.

SATURDAY
10

SUNDAY
11

AUGUST						
S	M	T	W	T	F	S
				1	2	3
4	5	6	7	8	9	10
11	12	13	14	15	16	17
18	19	20	21	22	23	24
25	26	27	28	29	30	31

AUGUST

TUESDAY
13

WEDNESDAY
14

THURSDAY
15

FRIDAY
16

SUMMER SUNFLOWER
by Ruby Hall, Vance, AL. 60" x 88". Ruby grew sunflowers for the first time and wanted to re-create them in fabric so she could enjoy them all winter long. A blue ribbon winner at the Enterprise Quilt Show, Enterprise, AL, and displayed at Quilting On The Farm, Geraldine, AL.

SATURDAY
17

SUNDAY
18

			AUGUST			
S	M	T	W	T	F	S
					1	2	3
4	5	6	7	8	9	10
11	12	13	14	15	16	17
18	19	20	21	22	23	24
25	26	27	28	29	30	31

AUGUST

MONDAY
19

TUESDAY
20

WEDNESDAY
21

THURSDAY
22

FRIDAY
23

SOUTHWEST BORDERS QUILT by Meg Zechiel, Tucson, AZ. 40" x 40". This is one of the 25 border swap quilts from the GEnie Online Quilters II Guild. Center block by Meg, borders added by Kathy Semone, Sandy Wheeler, Dorothy Buerkle, and Staci Emmons. The participants live across the country from California to Washington, DC, and most have never met except on the computer.

SATURDAY
24

SUNDAY
25

AUGUST						
S	M	T	W	T	F	S
				1	2	3
4	5	6	7	8	9	10
11	12	13	14	15	16	17
18	19	20	21	22	23	24
25	26	27	28	29	30	31

AUGUST / SEPTEMBER

MONDAY
26

TUESDAY
27

WEDNESDAY
28

THURSDAY
29

FRIDAY
30

OF WINE & ROSES
by Victoria L. Miller, Northfield, MN. 84" x 100". This pattern by Pat Cox was inspired by Mrs. S. J. Soden's 1935 quilt titled "Kansas." Victoria's updated version uses the brightly colored 1990s fabrics and has many more grapes and roses. Best of Show winner at the Minnesota State Fair.

SATURDAY
31

SUNDAY
1

SEPTEMBER						
S	M	T	W	T	F	S
1	2	3	4	5	6	7
8	9	10	11	12	13	14
15	16	17	18	19	20	21
22	23	24	25	26	27	28
29	30					

I like this quilt, the colors are so vibrant and full of life. It looks like a face on the trunk of the tree. Which to me symbolizes how your life should be, strong and true to yourself and the ones you love. But the branches of gold spreading, weaving and branching off are the interesting part of life. Life's little adventure failures, accomplishments, happiness, sorrows, and loves we've experienced.

If any quilt should be called "The Tree of Life." It is this one!

SEPTEMBER

MONDAY   LABOR DAY

2

TUESDAY

3

WEDNESDAY

4

THURSDAY

5

FRIDAY

6

QUANTUM LEAP
by Nancy Jerauld, Belfast, ME.
54" x 40". Focus on color rather
than pattern in the fabric is what
gave Nancy the freedom to
create this piece. Nancy machine
quilted in rayon thread,
embellished the tree trunk crazy
quilt style, and used the
couching technique for the
branches. Displayed at New
England Images IV and AQS.

SATURDAY

7

SUNDAY

8

			SEPTEMBER			
S	M	T	W	T	F	S
1	2	3	4	5	6	7
8	9	10	11	12	13	14
15	16	17	18	19	20	21
22	23	24	25	26	27	28
29	30					

SEPTEMBER

MONDAY

9

TUESDAY

10

WEDNESDAY

11

THURSDAY

12

FRIDAY

13

MIGRATING SOUTH
by Nadine Moss, Grove, OK. 54"
x 75". All the birds are different!
Seventy-two fabrics are
represented in the birds only.
Running out of a background
(white on white) was not the
disaster it seemed, it just made
Nadine move in a more creative
direction and use many of the
neutrals. Displayed at Grove
Quilt Show, and Ozark
Piecemakers Quilt Show,
Springfield, MO.

SATURDAY   ROSH HASHANAH

14

SUNDAY

15

SEPTEMBER

S	M	T	W	T	F	S
1	2	3	4	5	6	7
8	9	10	11	12	13	14
15	16	17	18	19	20	21
22	23	24	25	26	27	28
29	30					

SEPTEMBER

MONDAY
16

TUESDAY
17

WEDNESDAY
18

THURSDAY
19

FRIDAY
20

KALEIDOSCOPE
by Dixie R. Waltimyer, Candler,
NC. 107" x 178". "When plaid
was a rage, I accumulated yards
and yards. It was a challenge to
use it in an approiate manner."
Check out the matching of the
plaid lines! A winner at the
Asheville Quilt Guild Show,
Asheville, NC.

SATURDAY
21

SUNDAY
22

			SEPTEMBER			
S	M	T	W	T	F	S
1	2	3	4	5	6	7
8	9	10	11	12	13	14
15	16	17	18	19	20	21
22	23	24	25	26	27	28
29	30					

SEPTEMBER

23

TUESDAY

24

WEDNESDAY

25

THURSDAY

26

FRIDAY

27

GARDEN SUNSET
by Vicky Slater, Wisconsin
Rapids, WI. 86" x 90". Vicky
bought lots of eighths and
quarter yards of fabric for a
workshop. When people there
wondered how she could
possibly use them all, Vicky took
it as a dare! This quilt has all the
fabrics she could fit into it! This
dare resulted in ribbons at Star
Point Quilters Guild Show,
Stevens Point, WI, and Darting
Needles Quilt Guild Show,
Appleton, WI.

SATURDAY

28

SUNDAY

29

SEPTEMBER

S	M	T	W	T	F	S
1	2	3	4	5	6	7
8	9	10	11	12	13	14
15	16	17	18	19	20	21
22	23	24	25	26	27	28
29	30					

SEPTEMBER / OCTOBER

MONDAY

30

TUESDAY

1

WEDNESDAY

2

THURSDAY

3

FRIDAY

4

HOORAY FOR CAPTAIN SPAULDING or WHERE'S HARPO? by James Tucker, Madison, WI. 56" x 56". Traditional blocks fashioned from non-traditional fabrics form this kinetic baby quilt. Jim's nephew, Frank, matches the quilt in energy. Completed just in time for publication.

SATURDAY

5

SUNDAY

6

OCTOBER

S	M	T	W	T	F	S
		1	2	3	4	5
6	7	8	9	10	11	12
13	14	15	16	17	18	19
20	21	22	23	24	25	26
27	28	29	30	31		

OCTOBER

MONDAY
7

TUESDAY
8

WEDNESDAY
9

THURSDAY
10

FRIDAY
11

COMPASS OF LIFE
by Maria Chisnall, Nassau, Bahamas. 48" in diameter. Made as a part of the Androsia Challenge held in Nassau and inspired by local batiked fabrics (Androsia). The colors and design depict the beautiful waters of the islands. Displayed at Quilter's Heritage Celebration, Lancaster, PA.

SATURDAY
12

SUNDAY
13

OCTOBER

S	M	T	W	T	F	S
		1	2	3	4	5
6	7	8	9	10	11	12
13	14	15	16	17	18	19
20	21	22	23	24	25	26
27	28	29	30	31		

OCTOBER

MONDAY   COLUMBUS DAY
14

TUESDAY
15

WEDNESDAY
16

THURSDAY
17

FRIDAY
18

MIGRATION
by Johanna Chellis, Wayne, ME. 60" x 78". October in Maine is the inspiration for this quilt. The black triangles represent geese flying across New England hillsides. Vermont Quilt Festival and Maine Quilts IV awarded prizes to this piece.

SATURDAY
19

SUNDAY
20

OCTOBER

S	M	T	W	T	F	S
		1	2	3	4	5
6	7	8	9	10	11	12
13	14	15	16	17	18	19
20	21	22	23	24	25	26
27	28	29	30	31		

OCTOBER

TUESDAY
22

WEDNESDAY
23

THURSDAY
24

FRIDAY
25

ALMOST AMISH
by Barb Mechura, Faribault, MN. 38" x 48". Barb loves Amish quilts, but the contemporary in her won't let it happen. This is as close as she could come! Each color was treated as a seperate piece with different quilting designs. Blue ribbon winner in the Original Design Wall Hanging catagory at the Minnesota State Fair.

SATURDAY
26

SUNDAY
27

OCTOBER

S	M	T	W	T	F	S
		1	2	3	4	5
6	7	8	9	10	11	12
13	14	15	16	17	18	19
20	21	22	23	24	25	26
27	28	29	30	31		

OCTOBER / NOVEMBER

MONDAY

28

TUESDAY

29

WEDNESDAY

30

THURSDAY   **HALLOWEEN**

31

FRIDAY

1

SUNSET, CORAL AND COTTON CANDY by Lynn M. Ticotsky, Cincinnati, OH. 93" x 93". The end product of a 12-week workshop focused on honing technical skills and innovative design used in quiltmaking produced this sampler. Displayed at NQA, Charleston, WV.

SATURDAY

2

SUNDAY

3

			NOVEMBER			
S	M	T	W	T	F	S
					1	2
3	4	5	6	7	8	9
10	11	12	13	14	15	16
17	18	19	20	21	22	23
24	25	26	27	28	29	30

NOVEMBER

MONDAY

4

TUESDAY

5

WEDNESDAY

6

THURSDAY

7

FRIDAY

8

MARINER'S COMPASS
by Betsy Wallace, Alanson, MI.
56" x 70". Hand piecing and hand
quilting are used to acheive the
clean, precise look of this quilt.
Compass points are used as the
design element of choice in the
border. Displayed at NQA,
Charleston, WV.

SATURDAY

9

SUNDAY

10

NOVEMBER

S	M	T	W	T	F	S
					1	2
3	4	5	6	7	8	9
10	11	12	13	14	15	16
17	18	19	20	21	22	23
24	25	26	27	28	29	30

NOVEMBER

MONDAY   VETERANS' DAY
11

TUESDAY
12

WEDNESDAY
13

THURSDAY
14

FRIDAY
15

LINCOLN QUILT
by Maxine Bossing, Springfield, MO. 90" x 113". The 4,016 squares (not counting the border) were all scissors cut, hand pieced, and hand quilted. Maxine says that Abraham Lincoln's mother made him a quilt like this the year he was born. A viewer's choice winner at Ozark Peacemakers Quilt Guild Show, Springfield, MO.

SATURDAY
16

SUNDAY
17

NOVEMBER

S	M	T	W	T	F	S
					1	2
3	4	5	6	7	8	9
10	11	12	13	14	15	16
17	18	19	20	21	22	23
24	25	26	27	28	29	30

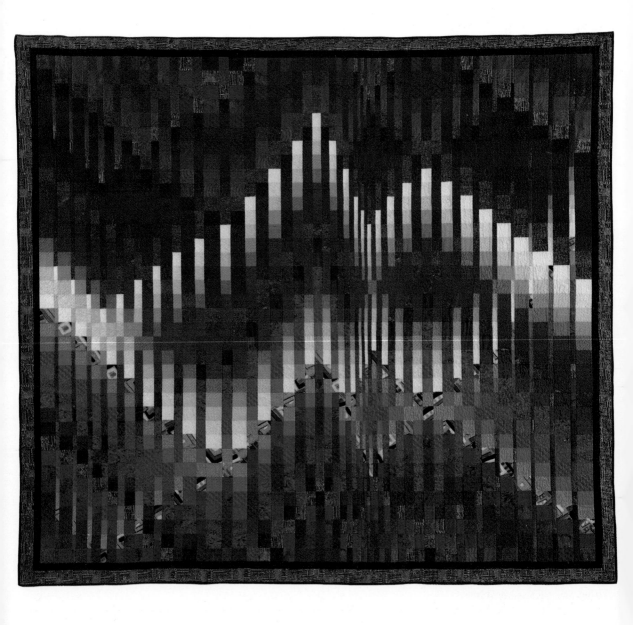

NOVEMBER

MONDAY
18

TUESDAY
19

WEDNESDAY
20

THURSDAY
21

FRIDAY
22

WELCOME
by Virginia Holloway, Randolph, MA. 89" x 78". Happy colors and the endless possibilities of bargello were Virginia's motivating forces for this variation on a theme. A winner at the Asheville, NC, Quilt Show. Displayed at PNQE and Pacific International Quit Show, San Francisco, CA.

SATURDAY
23

SUNDAY
24

			NOVEMBER			
S	M	T	W	T	F	S
					1	2
3	4	5	6	7	8	9
10	11	12	13	14	15	16
17	18	19	20	21	22	23
24	25	26	27	28	29	30

NOVEMBER / DECEMBER

MONDAY
25

TUESDAY
26

WEDNESDAY
27

THURSDAY   THANKSGIVING DAY
28

FRIDAY
29

FRIENDSHIP BASKETS
by East Cobb Quilter's Guild, Marietta, GA. 80" x 103". This piece was made for Alice Berg as outgoing president by her guild. Each member was asked to make a basket block of their choice and then they were creatively made into a quilt by Mary Ellen Von Holt and Barbara Butler. Machine quilted by Karen Fuller. Displayed at Georgia Celebrates Quilts, Marietta, GA, and Quilt Show On The Farm, Geraldine, AL.

SATURDAY
30

SUNDAY
1

DECEMBER						
S	M	T	W	T	F	S
1	2	3	4	5	6	7
8	9	10	11	12	13	14
15	16	17	18	19	20	21
22	23	24	25	26	27	28
29	30	31				

DECEMBER

MONDAY

2

TUESDAY

3

WEDNESDAY

4

THURSDAY

5

FRIDAY   **HANUKKAH**

6

JANETTE'S TULIP BASKETS
by Janette Meetze, Bixby, OK.
60" x 75". Precise machine
piecing, fine hand appliqué, and
hand quilting combine to finish
this traditional beauty. A blue
ribbon winner at the Green
County Quilter's Guild Show,
Tulsa, OK.

SATURDAY

7

SUNDAY

8

DECEMBER

S	M	T	W	T	F	S
1	2	3	4	5	6	7
8	9	10	11	12	13	14
15	16	17	18	19	20	21
22	23	24	25	26	27	28
29	30	31				

DECEMBER

MONDAY

9

TUESDAY

10

WEDNESDAY

11

THURSDAY

12

FRIDAY

13

ESSENCE OF WINTER
by Doris McManus, Pleasanton, CA. 45" x 53". Doris's original design captures the feeling of a bright cold winter day after a snow storm. Trees made from lace and hand-dyed fabrics create the cool landscape. First place winner at the Alameda County Fair and a winner at the Marin Quilt Show.

SATURDAY

14

SUNDAY

15

DECEMBER						
S	M	T	W	T	F	S
1	2	3	4	5	6	7
8	9	10	11	12	13	14
15	16	17	18	19	20	21
22	23	24	25	26	27	28
29	30	31				

DECEMBER

MONDAY
16

TUESDAY
17

WEDNESDAY
18

THURSDAY
19

FRIDAY
20

NORTHERN LIGHTS
by Mary Field, Asheville, NC. 56" x 78". 1000 Pyramid-pattern used in non-traditional colors to create stars. It took more than 800 triangles to achieve this effect. Displayed at NQA, Charleston, WV, and the Mid-Atlantic Quilt Festival, Williamsburg, VA.

SATURDAY
21

SUNDAY
22

DECEMBER						
S	M	T	W	T	F	S
1	2	3	4	5	6	7
8	9	10	11	12	13	14
15	16	17	18	19	20	21
22	23	24	25	26	27	28
29	30	31				

DECEMBER

MONDAY
23

TUESDAY
24

WEDNESDAY CHRISTMAS
25

THURSDAY
26

FRIDAY
27

RAMBLING ROSES STAINED GLASS by Shirley M. Barrett, Lakeside, MT. 50" x 72". Machine stippling and trapunto in the flowers are techniques unusual to the stained glass genre. The marbelized fabric provided the realistic look of the glass. Viewer's Choice and first place winner at the Flathead Quilters Guild Show, Kalispell, MT.

SATURDAY
28

SUNDAY
29

DECEMBER

S	M	T	W	T	F	S
1	2	3	4	5	6	7
8	9	10	11	12	13	14
15	16	17	18	19	20	21
22	23	24	25	26	27	28
29	30	31				

DECEMBER /JANUARY

MONDAY
30

TUESDAY
31

WEDNESDAY   NEW YEAR'S DAY
1

THURSDAY
2

FRIDAY
3

HEAVEN & EARTH
by Vicky Haider, Minot, ND. 42"
x 42". A pictorial version of the
pioneer braid is achieved with
careful color gradations. Front
piece for a one-woman show at
University Art Gallery, Minot,
and first place winner at Indian
Summer Quilt Show, Fargo, ND.

SATURDAY
4

SUNDAY
5

			JANUARY			
S	M	T	W	T	F	S
			1	2	3	4
5	6	7	8	9	10	11
12	13	14	15	16	17	18
19	20	21	22	23	24	25
26	27	28	29	30	31	

1996

JANUARY
S	M	T	W	T	F	S
	1	2	3	4	5	6
7	8	9	10	11	12	13
14	15	16	17	18	19	20
21	22	23	24	25	26	27
28	29	30	31			

FEBRUARY
S	M	T	W	T	F	S
				1	2	3
4	5	6	7	8	9	10
11	12	13	14	15	16	17
18	19	20	21	22	23	24
25	26	27	28	29		

MARCH
S	M	T	W	T	F	S
					1	2
3	4	5	6	7	8	9
10	11	12	13	14	15	16
17	18	19	20	21	22	23
24	25	26	27	28	29	30
31						

APRIL
S	M	T	W	T	F	S
	1	2	3	4	5	6
7	8	9	10	11	12	13
14	15	16	17	18	19	20
21	22	23	24	25	26	27
28	29	30				

MAY
S	M	T	W	T	F	S
			1	2	3	4
5	6	7	8	9	10	11
12	13	14	15	16	17	18
19	20	21	22	23	24	25
26	27	28	29	30	31	

JUNE
S	M	T	W	T	F	S
						1
2	3	4	5	6	7	8
9	10	11	12	13	14	15
16	17	18	19	20	21	22
23	24	25	26	27	28	29
30						

JULY
S	M	T	W	T	F	S
	1	2	3	4	5	6
7	8	9	10	11	12	13
14	15	16	17	18	19	20
21	22	23	24	25	26	27
28	29	30	31			

AUGUST
S	M	T	W	T	F	S
				1	2	3
4	5	6	7	8	9	10
11	12	13	14	15	16	17
18	19	20	21	22	23	24
25	26	27	28	29	30	31

SEPTEMBER
S	M	T	W	T	F	S
1	2	3	4	5	6	7
8	9	10	11	12	13	14
15	16	17	18	19	20	21
22	23	24	25	26	27	28
29	30					

OCTOBER
S	M	T	W	T	F	S
		1	2	3	4	5
6	7	8	9	10	11	12
13	14	15	16	17	18	19
20	21	22	23	24	25	26
27	28	29	30	31		

NOVEMBER
S	M	T	W	T	F	S
					1	2
3	4	5	6	7	8	9
10	11	12	13	14	15	16
17	18	19	20	21	22	23
24	25	26	27	28	29	30

DECEMBER
S	M	T	W	T	F	S
1	2	3	4	5	6	7
8	9	10	11	12	13	14
15	16	17	18	19	20	21
22	23	24	25	26	27	28
29	30	31				

1997

JANUARY
S	M	T	W	T	F	S
			1	2	3	4
5	6	7	8	9	10	11
12	13	14	15	16	17	18
19	20	21	22	23	24	25
26	27	28	29	30	31	

FEBRUARY
S	M	T	W	T	F	S
						1
2	3	4	5	6	7	8
9	10	11	12	13	14	15
16	17	18	19	20	21	22
23	24	25	26	27	28	

MARCH
S	M	T	W	T	F	S
						1
2	3	4	5	6	7	8
9	10	11	12	13	14	15
16	17	18	19	20	21	22
23	24	25	26	27	28	29
30	31					

APRIL
S	M	T	W	T	F	S
		1	2	3	4	5
6	7	8	9	10	11	12
13	14	15	16	17	18	19
20	21	22	23	24	25	26
27	28	29	30			

MAY
S	M	T	W	T	F	S
				1	2	3
4	5	6	7	8	9	10
11	12	13	14	15	16	17
18	19	20	21	22	23	24
25	26	27	28	29	30	31

JUNE
S	M	T	W	T	F	S
1	2	3	4	5	6	7
8	9	10	11	12	13	14
15	16	17	18	19	20	21
22	23	24	25	26	27	28
29	30					

JULY
S	M	T	W	T	F	S
		1	2	3	4	5
6	7	8	9	10	11	12
13	14	15	16	17	18	19
20	21	22	23	24	25	26
27	28	29	30	31		

AUGUST
S	M	T	W	T	F	S
					1	2
3	4	5	6	7	8	9
10	11	12	13	14	15	16
17	18	19	20	21	22	23
24	25	26	27	28	29	30
31						

SEPTEMBER
S	M	T	W	T	F	S
	1	2	3	4	5	6
7	8	9	10	11	12	13
14	15	16	17	18	19	20
21	22	23	24	25	26	27
28	29	30				

OCTOBER
S	M	T	W	T	F	S
			1	2	3	4
5	6	7	8	9	10	11
12	13	14	15	16	17	18
19	20	21	22	23	24	25
26	27	28	29	30	31	

NOVEMBER
S	M	T	W	T	F	S
						1
2	3	4	5	6	7	8
9	10	11	12	13	14	15
16	17	18	19	20	21	22
23	24	25	26	27	28	29
30						

DECEMBER
S	M	T	W	T	F	S
	1	2	3	4	5	6
7	8	9	10	11	12	13
14	15	16	17	18	19	20
21	22	23	24	25	26	27
28	29	30	31			

The American Quilter's Society

The American Quilter's Society was founded in 1984 to promote the accomplishments of today's quilter. Because of that goal, AQS now publishes *American Quilter* magazine, dozens of quilting books, and it holds a national quilt show and contest annually.

You can be a member of AQS for only $18.00 a year. Benefits include receiving a quarterly magazine full of informative quilting articles and full-color photographs, being able to buy quilt books at a substantial discount, having an outlet to sell quilts through the AQS quilt referral service, and having an opportunity to win thousands of dollars in the annual AQS Quilt Show & Contest in Paducah, Kentucky, in April. AQS periodically sends its members an *Update* newsletter and book order forms to keep them informed on Society news and savings on books.

Join AQS. You could save more than the $18.00 membership fee on your first book order! *American Quilter* magazine alone is worth it. Learn more about quilting and the latest techniques. Appreciate what the top quilt artists are doing and how they do it. Send in the coupon below.

I want to become a **MEMBER** of *American Quilter's Society* and receive all the benefits.

☐ (#2501) 1 yr. AQS membership – $18.00

☐ (#2502) 2 yr. AQS membership – $33.00 ($3.00 savings)

☐ (#2503) 3 yr. AQS membership – $49.00 ($5.00 savings)

Add $5.00 for Canadian postage. Add $10.00 for foreign airmail postage.

Name _____

Address _____

City _____ State _____ Zip _____

Method of Payment

☐ Check enclosed   ☐ Bill me   Charge my: ☐ VISA   ☐ MasterCard

If paying by charge card, please provide the following information:

Cardholder's name _____

Card number _____ MC Interbank No. _____

Expiration date _____ Signature _____

American Quilter's Society

P. O. Box 3290 • Paducah, KY 42002-3290

NOTES